D0853902

THE
WRIGHT
BROTHERS

Richard Tames

Franklin Watts
New York ● London ● Sydney ● Toronto

Contents

© 1990 Franklin Watts

Franklin Watts Inc.
387 Park Avenue South
New York
N.Y. 10016

Phototypeset by: JB Type, Hove, East Sussex
Printed in: Belgium
Series Editor: Hazel Poole
Editor: Dee Turner
Designed by: Nick Cannan

Tames, Richard.
    The Wright brothers / Richard Tames.
        p.   cm. — (Lifetimes)
    Summary: Discusses the Wright brothers' lifelong involvement with powered flight and their successful development of the first airplane.
    ISBN 0-531-14002-4
    1. Wright, Wilbur, 1867-1912—Juvenile literature. 2. Wright, Orville, 1871-1948—Juvenile literature. 3. Aeronautics—United States—Biography—Juvenile literature. [1. Wright, Wilbur, 1867-1912. 2. Wright, Orville, 1871-1948. 3. Aeronautics—Biography.] I. Title . II. Series: Lifetimes (London, England)
TL540.W7T36   1990
629.13'0092'2—dc20
[B]
[92]   89-29345
                                                            CIP
                                                            AC

The Bicycle Boys

In 1878 Bishop Milton Wright returned to his home after a business trip for the United Brethren Church. He brought with him a present for his young family — a toy helicopter. Many years later, Orville Wright remembered how their father came into the living room with a tiny object concealed in his hands:-

"Before we could see what it was he tossed it into the air. Instead of falling to the floor as we expected, it flew across the room until it struck the ceiling, where it fluttered a while and finally sank to the floor."

Orville and his elder brother Wilbur examined the toy with care. They found that it was made from cork, bamboo, and paper, with an "engine" driven by rubber bands. These were materials they could easily get for themselves. So they built a number of copies, gradually making them larger and larger. They were surprised and puzzled to find that, while the small ones flew successfully, the large ones would not. It would be many years before they would discover that a model only twice the size of the original would need *eight* times as much power to fly equally well.

In the Wright household, children were expected to find things out for themselves. As Orville Wright remembered it:-

" ... we were lucky enough to grow up in a home ... where there was always much encouragement to

Bishop Milton Wright, a father who encouraged curiosity.

children ... to investigate whatever aroused curiosity."

Susan Wright, the boys' mother, was one of those people who could "mend anything" and she often made toys for her family or tools to use in the kitchen or around the house. The boys followed her example. Wilbur invented a gadget for folding paper. Orville began making his own prints and woodcuts at the age of twelve. Together the brothers built their own lathe, for shaping pieces of wood.

Wilbur was a good student and an excellent athlete. He planned to follow in his father's footsteps, studying at Yale University and then becoming a minister of the Church. But a sports accident when he was eighteen changed the whole course of his life. Playing hockey one day, he was hit in the face by a wildly swung stick. He lost almost all of his upper teeth and several of the lower ones. Although his mouth gradually healed and surgery and false teeth restored the shape of his face, for a while he lost all his confidence. He suffered from constant stomach pains and came to believe that he had a weak heart. He gave up all thoughts of a career and stayed at home, helping around the house and reading quietly in his room.

Orville, meanwhile, turned his print-making hobby into a printing business. He began by publishing a newspaper for his classmates, then printed leaflets and posters for local storekeepers. Then he decided to build a much larger press out of secondhand parts begged or bought from professional printers. It turned out to be much more difficult than he had thought it would be. So he asked Wilbur to help him. Wilbur did. The result was success and a weekly neighborhood paper, *West Side News*, which Wilbur edited and Orville printed and sold. After a successful year the brothers upgraded it to become a four-page daily, *The Evening Item*. But this was too ambitious. It was impossible to compete with the big dailies in their home town of Dayton, Ohio.

The modern "safety bicycle" — basically unchanged in a century.

After four months the *Item* ceased publication.

Once again it was Orville who brought Wilbur out of his shell, this time by buying one of the new-fangled **"safety bicycles"** and becoming a keen competitor in local track competitions. Wilbur bought one, too, and went along to watch Orville compete. Both boys were first class practical mechanics and they soon saw a business opportunity in the craze for "wheeling." In 1892 they opened their own shop, selling and repairing bicycles. By 1896 the Wright Cycle Company was designing and manufacturing its own bicycles.

Wilbur, meanwhile, continued to read widely. In 1894 he read an article about a German engineer, Otto Lilienthal, who had made hundreds of short flights in a **glider** of his own design. Lilienthal's pioneering interest in **aviation** cost him his life when his glider crashed in August 1896. News of his dramatic death renewed Wilbur's interest in the problem of manned flight. He and Orville began to read

Orville (left), **although younger than Wilbur (right), took the lead in involving them both in a successful business (right) — a bicycle shop, now re-erected at Henry Ford's museum.**

everything they could find in local libraries about experiments in aviation. They also spent hours in the countryside watching bird flight through field glasses. The bicycle business proved to be ideally suited to their new interest. Busy during the good weather and slow in winter, it gave them spare time as well as money to devote to experiments.

Another aviation pioneer was Professor Samuel Langley, the secretary of the Smithsonian Institution in Washington, D.C. In 1896 he built and flew a small model plane which was powered by a tiny steam engine. It flew for just over a minute. Langley wrote about his experiment in a popular magazine in 1897 and later published a longer account entitled *Experiments in Aerodynamics*.

Having learned as much as they could on their own, the Wrights decided to contact Langley at the Smithsonian Institution for further advice. Wilbur wrote modestly:-

"I wish to obtain such papers as the Smithsonian Institution has published ... and if possible a list of other works in print in the English language. I am an enthusiast, but not a crank in the sense that I have some pet theories as to the proper construction of a flying machine. I wish to avail myself of all that is already known and then if possible add my mite to help on the future worker who will attain final success."

Flights of Fancy

For centuries, people had been fascinated by the idea of human flight. As early as 1250 an English monk, Roger Bacon, suggested it would be possible to build a heavier-than-air flying machine. About 250 years later, the Italian artist and inventor, Leonardo da Vinci, made sketches of flying machines. But it was not until the eighteenth century that model gliders and hot air balloons showed that flight was possible.

The true pioneer of the science of flight was a British inventor, Sir George Cayley. In 1796 he flew a model helicopter and in 1809 designed an unmanned full-size glider. He also designed the first **biplane** and in 1849 flew a glider carrying a ten-year-old boy.

The second half of the nineteenth century saw many inventions and discoveries in aviation. The invention of the **windtunnel**, Lilienthal's experiments with gliders, Chanute's study of the history of aviation, and Langley's model airplanes all helped pave the way for the Wright brothers' conquest of powered flight in 1903.

A Cayley design (above) **of 1799. Percy Pilcher** (below)**, the first Englishman to fly, was killed experimenting in 1899.**

The Flying Problem

By 1899, wide and careful reading had given the Wrights a good understanding of what they later called "the flying problem." There were two main issues: how to get the airplane off the ground, and then how to control its flight once you had got it airborne.

Professor Langley, among others, focused on the first issue — the problem of power. He worked on producing enough **thrust** (forward movement) and **lift** (upward movement) to enable a heavier-than-air machine to get off the ground. Experimenters such as Lilienthal were more concerned with the problem of control. For them, the problem was to maintain balance and direction while moving through air currents which could act on a machine in three dimensions at the same time.

The Wrights sided with Lilienthal and believed that the first problem to overcome was that of controlled flight. Only then could powered flight be attempted. So they decided to learn about flying by experimenting with gliders, and to concentrate on improving what the brilliant Lilienthal had achieved before his tragic death.

Lilienthal had found that sudden gusts of wind often lifted one wing higher than the other. If balance was not quickly restored, with the air currents flowing evenly over both wings, the glider would slip sideways and crash to the ground. Lilienthal's

Wright 1902 glider — note the tense, poised position of the "pilot" and reliance on man-handling.

answer was to throw his own body-weight from side to side to counteract the force of the wind. But this required great speed and strength, as well as skill in timing. The Wrights looked instead for a mechanical solution to the problem. They decided to try moving parts of the wing, so that the glider could be kept balanced on the air currents.

Wilbur found the answer when he remembered watching buzzards in flight, regaining their balance by twisting the tips of their wings. To test out his idea, he decided to build a kite with wings that could be "warped" or twisted at the tips, using cords. In August 1899, Wilbur tested the wing-warping kite in a field outside Dayton. It worked. The next step would be to build a glider that used the same principle, yet was big enough to carry a pilot.

Testing such a machine would be dangerous. So Wilbur wrote to the United States Weather Bureau for help in selecting the safest possible site. The Bureau suggested Kitty Hawk, a fishing village in sand dunes on an island off the coast of North Carolina. Wilbur wrote

The Wright 1902 glider (below and right) **airborne — note the campsite below.**

to the weather station there and received a reply from Joseph Dosher, the telegraph operator. He described the mile-wide beach as clear of trees and high hills for 37 km (60 miles) to the south, with prevailing winds from the north and northeast during September and October. He was sorry, but it would not be possible to rent a house. "So you will have to bring tents," he wrote.

Confident that they had taken an important step forward in mastering the problem of flight, the Wrights then contacted another aviation pioneer, Octave Chanute, a brilliant American engineer. Once again it was Wilbur who wrote the letter:-

"For some years I have been afflicted with the belief that flight is possible to men. My disease has increased in severity and I feel that it will soon cost me an increased amount of money, if not my life. I have been trying to arrange my affairs in such a way that I can devote my entire time for a few months to experiment in this field."

Wilbur then described the plan for a full-scale, warp-winged, man-carrying glider and asked Chanute for advice and suggestions. Chanute became an enthusiastic supporter of the Wrights' work.

The Wrights' man-carrying glider was assembled at Kitty Hawk at the end of September 1900. With a wingspan of about 5 m (17 ft), it was more than three times larger than their experimental kite. High winds forced them to fly it unmanned at

first. On October 10, disaster struck when a sudden gust snatched the glider from the ground and smashed it down 6 m (20 ft) away. Patiently the brothers picked up the shattered pieces and spent a week putting it back together again. Eventually they were able to make manned flights.

Sliding the glider down a 24-m (80 ft) sandhill into a facing wind, they could get enough lift to travel about 90–120 m (300–400 ft). Then they made a controlled landing, using a front-mounted horizontal **rudder** which the pilot moved up or down to control the flow of air over the machine. This prevented the sort of nose dive that had killed Lilienthal.

By July 1901, they were back again, this time with a glider larger and heavier than anyone had ever attempted to fly before. It took nine tries for Wilbur to find the right

Wright 1903 Flyer at the campsite at Kill Devil Hill.

place to lie along the lower wing. When he did, the glider flew 90m (300 ft). But later flights, now under the encouraging eye of Octave Chanute, threw up a new problem. So far the Wrights had been content to fly in a straight line. When they tried to change direction to left or right, they lost control of the glider. Puzzled, they returned home to Dayton in August. As they noted some years later:

" … the experiments of 1901 were far from encouraging … we saw that the calculations upon which all flying machines had been based were unreliable, and that all were simply groping in the dark. Having set out with absolute faith in the existing scientific data, we were driven to doubt one thing after another, till, finally, after two years of experiment, we cast it all aside."

The Wrights next decided to experiment with wing design. They tried out model **airfoils** of various shapes, placed at various angles to the wind. The first experiments were clever but crude, involving airfoils fixed to a horizontally turning bicycle wheel. Then they used a windtunnel, made out of a 46-cm (18 in) wooden box and a fan driven by a one horsepower gasoline engine. This was immediately so successful that they went on to build a 1.8 m (6 ft) windtunnel with a glass top and a homemade pressure gauge. With this they could measure the lift achieved by model wings of any size and shape. After weeks of experiments they had gathered vital data about the most effective shapes and sizes. Most importantly, they also discovered that Lilienthal's calculations, which they had been relying on, were "very seriously in error."

In September 1902, a new glider, incorporating this new knowledge, was tested at Kitty Hawk. But the control problem remained. On September 23, the machine suddenly bucked in the air, slipped sideways, and fell backwards, ending wing-down against a sand dune. Orville walked away from the wreck without a scratch, but it took three days to repair the damage to the glider. Weeks later, however, they solved the problem of side-slipping by replacing the fixed rear tail-fin with a movable rudder. With this they were able to set new records for time and distance. Wilbur managed a flight of almost 190 m (622½ ft) in 26 seconds. In three years the boys from Dayton had built the world's first practical, controllable glider. The next step would be powered flight itself.

Otto Lilienthal

When he was a boy, Otto Lilienthal had been fascinated by the soaring flight of the storks that nested around his village in Germany. Later, as an engineer, he made a scientific study of the idea of flight. He figured out, by experiment, that an aircraft's wings needed to be curved in cross-section. Only then could the air currents lift a craft off the ground. In 1889 he published his findings in *Birdflight as the Basis for Aviation*, with detailed tables showing how much lift was produced by wings with different types of curve. But he realized that only by taking to the air himself could he really learn the secrets of flight.

In 1891, he began to experiment with gliders in his backyard. By 1894 he could launch himself into the air from a hillside and glide for over 335 m (1100 ft). On August 9, 1896, one of these flights ended in disaster when a gust of wind made him lose control. The glider plunged to the ground. Lilienthal died the next day of a broken spine. His brave experiments had a profound influence on the Wright brothers.

Intrepid birdman, Otto Lilienthal on one of his last successful flights.

The First Powered Flight

The Wright brothers were nearing final success, but there were others, too, in the race to fly. In France, Ferdinand Ferbier was experimenting with gliders based on the descriptions Wilbur had given in a lecture to the Western Society of Engineers at Chicago in 1901. From Washington, Professor Langley wrote inviting the Wrights to tell him all about the way they controlled their glider. Wilbur, believing that Langley intended to steal their ideas for his own project, politely declined.

Meanwhile, they tried to find an engine for their aircraft. At first the Wrights thought they could order one easily from a motor car manufacturer, but none was willing or able to supply what they needed for the amount they could pay. So they designed an engine themselves and had it built by Charlie Taylor, the mechanic who looked after their bicycle shop. They literally designed it as they made it, as Taylor remembered:-

"One of us would sketch out the

part we were talking about on a piece of scratch paper and I'd pin the sketch over my bench."

Working from these rough designs, Taylor produced the 4-cylinder, 12 horsepower engine in just six weeks.

Wilbur and Orville, meanwhile, worked on the propellers. Again, they assumed this would be a straightforward matter. However, they found that the size and shape of existing propellers, made for ships, were based on trial and error, not scientific calculation. They simply had no time to waste learning from their mistakes. But the problem of designing the perfect propeller was enormously difficult:-

"With the machine moving forward, the air flying backward, the propellers turning sideways, and nothing standing still, it seemed impossible to find a starting point from which to trace the various simultaneous reactions."

Three months of painstaking calculations brought success in the end. As Orville wrote to a friend in June 1902:-

"We had been unable to find anything of value in any of the works to which we had access, so we worked out a theory of our own on the subject and soon discovered, as we usually do, that all the propellers built heretofore, are *all wrong*."

Moment of disaster — Langley's "Aerodrome" nose-dives.

When the Wrights returned to Kitty Hawk in September 1903, they began their trails by practicing hovering in the 1902 glider. Their aim now was not to cover distance but to see how long they could stay in the air. Within days they were making glides lasting more than a minute.

When they began to assemble their plane, a fierce storm beat at the walls of the shed they had built to work in and threatened to rip off its roof. It was October by now, and winter was approaching. In Washington, Professor Langley was arranging a test flight for his own full-scale plane, which he called the Aerodrome. It proved to be a flop. Wilbur wrote to Chanute, saying

Take-Off! Wilbur (right) **sees Orville fly into history.**

that, after Langley's failure, it seemed to be "our turn to throw now and I wonder what our luck will be."

Then they heard that Langley was going to ask for more government money so that he could go on with his Aerodrome project. This news made the brothers change their plans at once. They had intended to try out the new 1903 machine as a glider first of all, mounting the engine only when sure that the frame was airworthy. Now, spurred on by the fear that Langley might, after all, beat them into the air, they decided to press straight ahead with an attempt at powered flight.

Orville (left) and Wilbur (right) worked as a natural team, each encouraging the other.

But first they had to test the engine. The first trials, on November 5, could hardly have been more discouraging. The engine backfired and gave out. The propellers would not revolve smoothly. Finally they jerked loose altogether, damaging their shafts, which had to be sent back to Dayton for Charlie Taylor to repair. Fresh trials on November 28 revealed a crack in one of the mended shafts. Orville rushed back to Dayton to get entirely new shafts made of solid spring steel.

Meanwhile, in Washington, Professor Langley made a second attempt to launch the Aerodrome. This also ended in disaster when its launch gear snagged on take-off, plunging the machine, a crippled wreck, into the icy waters of the Potomac River. The *New York Times* noted coldly that:-

"The ridiculous fiasco which attended the attempt at aerial navigation in the Langley flying machine was not unexpected. The flying machine that will really fly might be evolved by the combined and continuous efforts of mathematicians and mechanicians in from one to 10 million years."

Undaunted, Orville returned to Kitty Hawk with the new propeller shafts on December 11. On Monday, the 14th, the Wrights were at last ready to make their first attempt. However, unused to the power supplied by an engine, Wilbur lost

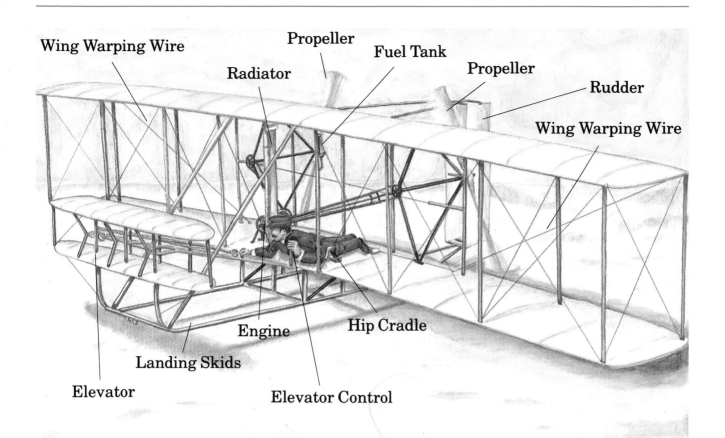

Wing Warping Wire

Propeller

Radiator

Fuel Tank

Propeller

Rudder

Wing Warping Wire

Engine

Hip Cradle

Landing Skids

Elevator

Elevator Control

control and the 32 m (105 ft) "flight" ended after 3½ seconds. But the Wrights were not downcast:-

"It was a nice easy landing for the operator. The power is ample and, but for a trifling error due to lack of experience with this machine and this method of starting, the machine would undoubtedly have flown beautifully. There is now no question of final success."

Minor repairs and a lack of wind delayed a second attempt until the morning of Thursday, the 17th. Now it was Orville's turn. Dressed in a business suit, complete with tie, starched collar and peaked cap, he lay along the lower wing of the machine. It was 10:35 a.m. As he released the wire that anchored the

Flyer I — frail-looking but practical, it set the style for twenty years.

craft, it moved slowly forward into an opposing wind of 43 kph (27 mph). After it had gone about 12 m (40 ft) and was traveling at just over 11 kph (7 mph), Orville pulled the **elevator** control and the airplane rose suddenly into the air. About 3 m (10 ft) above the ground it dipped, rose again, and then finally came down to settle on the ground just over 36 m (120 ft) from its take-off point. It had flown no further than the length of the cabin of a modern jumbo jet, and had been airborne for just 12 seconds. But it was the first manned, powered, controlled flight in history.

Octave Chanute

Chanute, born in France, emigrated to the United States as a child. There he trained as a civil engineer, constructing railways, buildings and bridges. He took a special interest in the damage that strong winds could do to buildings. This led him to study aerodynamics and the possibility of flight. By the 1890s, he had become an international expert on the history of flying.

In the 1890s, Chanute published a book called *Progress in Flying Machines*, which described the many flying experiments that had already taken place. By 1894, he was himself testing experimental gliders. In 1896 he succeeded in flying a man-carrying glider for 35 m (116 ft). When the Wright brothers wrote to him in 1900, he became their keen supporter. He also helped to make their work better known around the world. In later years, however, he was critical of them. He believed they had failed to recognize the important contribution his work made to their success.

Octave Chanute — his advice, encouragement and publicity were valuable to the Wrights, but his own experiments (below) **led nowhere.**

Flying in Circles

Orville Wright's historic 12-second flight, on December 17, 1903, was not the only flight the Wrights made that day. Three more times that morning the brothers took to the air, covering a greater distance each time. On the final flight Wilbur remained airborne for almost a minute and covered a distance of nearly 260 m (852 ft). But he landed awkwardly, damaging the craft slightly. And then, before any repairs could be made, a sudden savage gust of wind hurled the machine along the beach. It rolled over and over, until it was smashed so badly that repairing it immediately was out of the question.

Accounts of the Wrights' achievement did appear in the newspapers the following day, though they were far from accurate. The *Dayton Evening Herald* called their machine an **airship** and the *Virginian Pilot* claimed that it had traveled 4.8 km (3 miles) with "No Balloon Attached to Aid it." In January 1904, the Wrights issued a brief public statement, correcting press misinformation but refusing to give out any pictures or detailed

Preserved for posterity — Flyer I in a museum setting.

descriptions of the machine. The plane, now appropriately known as Flyer I, was crated up and put in storage. Work began on Flyer II.

Now that they had worked out the principles involved in building a practical airplane; the Wrights no longer needed the wide, windy spaces and soft beaches at Kitty Hawk. They found a new site for their operations at Huffman Prairie, a large field on a dairy farm near Dayton, and within sight of convenient transportation. Here they built a wooden **hangar**, in which they completed the building of Flyer II, commuting to the site each day by tram.

On two occasions toward the end of May 1904, newspaper reporters were invited to witness the trial flights of Flyer II. But bad weather meant that it could manage only a feeble 9 m (30 ft). The disillusioned pressmen decided flying was still no more than an amusing fad for cranks and not a practical form of transportation, much less a

Flight into history — markers chart the historic flight path.

A risky business — early flying needed luck and skill as well as sound design.

revolutionary one.

Throughout the summer of 1904, the Wrights continued to test and refine Flyer II, achieving flights of up to 427 m (1400 ft). In September, Wilbur flew in a complete circle for the first time, covering a recordbreaking distance of 1.2 km (¾ of a mile). And this time there was a witness to his success.

Amos T. Root, a bee-keeper and the publisher of a magazine with the curious title of *Gleanings in Bee Culture*, had driven to Huffman Prairie to watch the flight. Writing in the January, 1905 issue of his magazine, he described his reactions. It is the first-ever published eyewitness account of an

airplane flight:

"I have a wonderful story to tell you — a story that, in some respects, outrivals the Arabian Nights fables … God in his great mercy has permitted me to be, at least somewhat, instrumental in ushering in and introducing to the great wide world an invention that may outrank electric cars, automobiles, and all other methods of travel, and one which may fairly take a place beside the telephone and wireless telegraphy … it was my privilege … to see the first successful trip of an airship, without a balloon to sustain it, that the world has ever made, that is, to turn corners and come back to the starting point … The

Later developments enabled the pilot to sit at the controls.

operator takes his place lying flat on his face. This position offers less resistance to the wind. The engine is started and brought up to speed. The machine is held until ready to start by a sort of trap to be sprung when all is ready; then with a tremendous flapping and snapping of the four-cylinder engine, the huge machine springs aloft. When it first turned that circle, and came near the starting point, I was right in front of it … it was one of the grandest sights … of my life. Imagine a locomotive that has left its track, and is climbing up in the air right toward you — a locomotive without any wheels … but with white wings … Well, now, imagine this white locomotive, with wings that spread twenty feet each way, coming right toward you with a tremendous flap of its propellers, and you will have something like what I saw.

"When Columbus discovered America he did not know what the outcome would be and no one at that time knew … In a like manner these two brothers have probably not even a faint glimpse of what their discovery is going to bring to the children of men."

Flyer II was followed in June, 1905, by Flyer III, the world's first completely practical airplane. The autumn trials of that year set one new distance record after another until, on October 5, the plane flew almost 39 km (24 miles) in 38 minutes and 3 seconds.

Confident that the years of experimenting were now over, the Wrights wrote to the United States Secretary of War, offering to build an airplane for the Army to use to spy on the enemy in wartime. Amos T. Root had recognized the enormous importance of the flying machine he had witnessed, but at first the Army did not. They turned down the offer.

Fatal flight — cameras record Lathan's doomed Channel attempt.

The French Connection

In France, interest in aviation was especially keen. In 1783, the Montgolfier brothers had led the way, demonstrating the world's first hot air balloon, in which two men had flown as passengers. In 1852 the French had already established the world's first aeronautical society. The French achieved many other aviation "firsts." Here are some of them:

1909

First flight across the English Channel, made by Louis Blériot.

First air race held at Reims (won by an American, Glenn Curtis).

First death of a pilot in an air crash (Eugène Lefebvre, testing a Wright Type A in France).

1910

First country to issue pilots' licenses.

First aerial **reconnaissance** flight: two French Army officers flew 145 km (90 miles) in 2½ hours, taking photographs.

First twin-engined plane.

First fighter aircraft — a Voisin biplane fitted with a machine gun.

1911

First non-stop flight from London to Paris.

1913

Adolphe Pégoud becomes the first to use a parachute, and the first to fly a plane upside down.

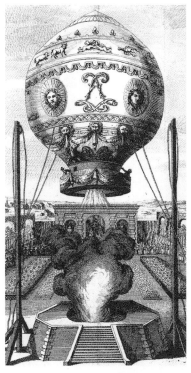

(Above) **The hot air Montgolfier balloon rises (1783). Blériot (left, hands on hips) poses beside his plane which landed, not crashed, near Dover Castle, England.**

The Age of Flight

In 1907, the Wrights went to Europe to discuss the possibility of selling their aircraft there. While in Paris they met Lieutenant Frank P. Lahm, an American army officer and keen balloonist. He quickly became a good friend and an enthusiastic supporter of their efforts to sell a "flying machine" to the United States Army. When he was transferred from the cavalry to the Signals Corps, he got an appointment for Wilbur to put his case before the committee that bought military equipment. The result of that meeting was an order from the Signal Corps for one flying machine, capable of carrying two men at 64 kph (40 mph).

In 1908, Wilbur Wright returned to Europe. On August 8, near Le Mans in France, he made the first demonstration flight of a Wright plane outside America. It caused enormous excitement. A month later, on the other side of the Atlantic, Orville completed the first trial flight of the 1908 Wright

(Left) **The Wright Military Flyer's test flight at Fort Myer, Virginia.**

Military specifications required the Wright plane to be easily transportable (below).

The crash that killed Lieutenant Selfridge.

Military Flyer at Fort Myer, Virginia. Two weeks after that, however, on September 17, disaster struck. Orville was making another test flight, with Lieutenant Thomas Selfridge as a passenger, when a propeller broke and the plane went out of control. The crash killed Selfridge and seriously injured Orville.

The next year saw further demonstration flights in France and Italy, and the signing of several contracts to build planes. On their return to America, the Wrights found themselves the stars of a huge celebration put on by their hometown of Dayton. At last people were realizing the importance of what they had done. The two-day festival consisted of three parades, a huge banquet and, with an audience of 2,000 schoolchildren, the public presentation of medals. Finally,

there was an enormous fireworks display showing images of Wilbur and Orville against the background of an American flag.

The Wrights said a polite "Thank You" and got back to work, demonstrating the 1909 Military Flyer to the satisfaction of the Army, which put it into service in August of that year. Frank Lahm became one of the United States' first official military pilots.

By that time Orville was in Germany, flying in Count Zeppelin's airship and being dined by **Kaiser** Wilhelm II. He also gave a series of demonstration flights for the German Army's top generals. Like previous demonstrations in France and Italy, these exhibitions were only for the chosen few. Then, on

October 4, Wilbur gave the first demonstration of flying before a mass audience. This took place in New York, where Wilbur flew along the Hudson River from Governor's Island to Grant's tomb and back again, a total of almost 68 km (42 miles). More than a million New Yorkers watched in wonder.

Aviation now began to become big business. In October, Wilbur started to instruct the first group of Army aviators, and in November "The Wright Company" was formed to manufacture planes. It had capital of $1,000,000; Wilbur was President. In an article Orville wrote:-

"I firmly believe in the future of the airplane for commerce, to carry mail, to carry passengers ... I cannot but believe that we stand at the beginning of a new era, the Age of Flight, and that the beginnings of today will be mightily overshadowed by the complete successes of tomorrow."

Royal approval (above), **the Wright Brothers with King Edward VII. Taking no chances** (below), **Wilbur flies across the Hudson with an emergency canoe.**

The Wright Company became known as the Dayton-Wright Company in 1917.

In October, flying a Wright Baby Grand, Orville set a new record with a speed of more than 112 kph (70 mph). In the same year the "Wright Exhibition Company" earned over $1,000,000 by organizing flying displays. Former President Theodore Roosevelt took to the air as a passenger in a Wright plane. In 1911 Orville completed the test flights of the Model B-1, which was taken into service by the United States Navy.

In October of that year, he returned to his old interest in gliding and at Kitty Hawk set a world soaring record of 9 minutes 45 seconds, which remained for the next ten years. In the same year, Galbraith Perry Rodgers flew a Wright plane from New York to California, taking three months, 70

Pathfinder — the Wright 1909 flier.

Still in step — the Wright Brothers in 1910.

landings, and a total flying time of 82 hours 4 minutes. Success, fame and fortune seemed to be the Wrights' just reward for their perseverance and courage.

Then came tragedy. On May 2, 1912, Wilbur was taken ill in Boston. He returned at once to Dayton, where his illness was diagnosed as **typhoid** fever. On May 30, he died.

Orville Wright lived on until 1948 and became the grand old man of American aviation. For a few years after Wilbur's death he continued to experiment with **seaplanes**, but he made his last flight as a pilot in 1918. Most of the rest of his career was spent as a consultant aeronautics engineer.

Tributes continued to be made to the pioneering achievements of the Wright brothers. In October 1927, the United States Army Air Corps dedicated Wright Field at Dayton, Ohio, as a major center for research work on aircraft design. On December 17, 1928, the 25th anniversary of the first-ever flight, the cornerstone of a monument to the Wright brothers was laid at Kitty Hawk. The huge granite memorial was completed in 1932 and unveiled by a woman pilot, Ruth Nichols. Its inscription reads:-

"In commemoration of the conquest of the air by the brothers Wilbur and Orville Wright. Conceived by genius. Achieved by dauntless resolution and unconquerable faith."

The Wright Brothers' National Memorial at Kitty Hawk.

Find Out More ...

Important Books

Epic Flights: Trailblazing Air Routes by David Jefferis; 1988, Franklin Watts.

The First Flyers: Pioneers of Aviation by David Jefferis; 1988, Franklin Watts.

One Day at Kitty Hawk by John Evangelist Walsh; 1975, Thomas Y. Crowell.

Wilbur and Orville Wright: The Flight to Adventure by Louis Sabin; 1983, Troll.

The Wright Brothers by Quentin Reynolds; 1981, Random House.

The Wright Brothers at Kitty Hawk by Donald J. Sobol; 1987, Scholastic.

The Wright Brothers: Heirs of Prometheus, Richard P. Hallion ed.; 1979, Smithsonian.

Important Addresses

The Henry Ford Museum
  Dearborn
  Michigan
  USA

National Air and Space Museum
  Smithsonian Institution
  Washington DC 20560
  USA

The Wright Brothers National Memorial
  Big Kill Devil Hill
  Kitty Hawk
  N Carolina
  USA

Important Dates

1867 Birth of Wilbur Wright
1871 Birth of Orville Wright
1878 Wright Brothers experiment with toy helicopters
1896 They design and manufacture bicycles
1897 They begin research into problems of flight
1899 They contact Smithsonian Institution and United States Weather Bureau
      Wilbur invents wing-warping
1900 Glider tests at Kitty Hawk
1901 Chanute witnesses glider tests
      Windtunnel experiments
1903 Wrights achieve first successful controlled powered flight in history
1904 Flyer II tested
      Amos T. Root witnesses first flight in a circle
1905 Flyer III – the world's first practical airplane
1907 United States army orders a Wright plane
1908 Wright plane demonstrated in France
1909 Dayton honors the Wrights
      United States army accepts Military Flyer into service
      Wilbur gives public flying display in New York
1911 Orville sets new records in flying at speed and soaring
1912 Death of Wilbur Wright
1932 Dedication of Kitty Hawk monument
1948 Death of Orville Wright

Glossary

Airfoil The cross-section shape of a wing. Airfoils have to be curved to allow the air currents to lift aircraft off the ground.

Airship A gas filled balloon driven by an engine and steered by a crew.

Aviation The science of flying.

Biplane An airplane with two sets of wings, one above the other.

Elevator A movable part of an aircraft that enables the pilot to make the plane climb or dive.

Glider An aircraft that rides on air currents and has no engine.

Hangar A building in which aircraft are stored or built.

Kaiser The title given to the German Emperor.

Lift The power that gives an aircraft its upward movement.

Reconnaissance A study or survey, usually of enemy territory in wartime.

Rudder A movable part of an aircraft that enables the pilot to steer left and right.

Safety bicycle The name given to the modern-style bicycle, with equal-sized wheels, when it was first invented. It was called this because it was safer to ride than previous models.

Seaplanes Airplanes fitted with floats so they can take off and land on water.

Thrust The power that gives an aircraft its forward movement.

Typhoid A feverish illness, at one time often fatal.

Wind tunnel A device for testing the way air flows over objects.

Index

Picture Acknowledgements

The publishers would like to thank the following for providing the photographs and illustrations in this book:
BBC Hulton Picture Library (*cover*, left) 16 (right), 21, 27 (bottom); Flight magazine 23 (bottom); The Mansell Collection *frontispiece*, 15, 26, 27 (top), 31; Mary Evans Picture Library 5; TRH Pictures 7, 9, 10, 11, 12, 18, 19, 20, 22, 24, 25, 28, 29 (bottom); The Science Museum (*cover*, right) 16 (left), 23 (top); Topham Picture Library 29 (top); US Navy 14; Wayland Picture Library 4, 6, 8, 13. The illustration on page 17 is by Nick Cannan.